Parakeets

Clive Harper and Beverley Randell

Contents

What parakeets look like	2
Parakeets' beaks	6
Parakeets' food	8
Tame parakeets and water	9
Hen birds and cock birds	10
Nests, eggs, and baby birds	11
Tame pet parakeets	15
Talking parakeets	16
Index	17

What parakeets look like

These birds are wild parakeets.
They are green with yellow heads.
They have black spots
on their necks.

Some pet parakeets are green, too.
They look like wild parakeets.
Other pet parakeets are blue or yellow or white.

Are wild parakeets green and yellow?

Yes. Wild parakeets are green and yellow.

A parakeet has two eyes
and a beak.
It has two feet with claws.
It has two wings
and a long tail,
and it has feathers
to keep it warm.
Parakeets have ears,
but you cannot see them.
They are hidden under
the feathers.

Do parakeets have ears?

Parakeets' beaks

Parakeets' beaks help them to open seeds.

Pet parakeets climb around inside their cages. Their beaks help them. Parakeets climb with their beaks and with their feet.

Yes. Parakeets have ears.
They are hidden under the feathers.

How do parakeets climb?

Parakeets' food

Pet parakeets eat birdseed.

They like apples
and carrots
and lettuce,
and they like
green dandelion leaves.

Parakeets drink clean water.

They climb with their beaks and their feet.

Tame parakeets and water

Some parakeets like having warm baths.

This parakeet flies to the sink when the water is running. She likes playing in the water.

Do parakeets eat seeds?

Hen birds and cock birds

Mother parakeets are called hen parakeets.
Father parakeets are called cock parakeets.

cock 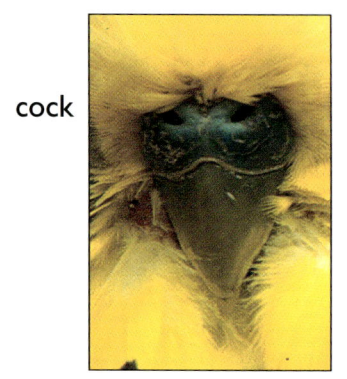  hen

A cock parakeet has
a blue patch
above its beak.
A hen parakeet
has a brown patch.

Yes. Parakeets do eat seeds.

Nests, eggs, and baby birds

All baby birds come from eggs.

Wild parakeets lay their eggs in holes in trees. They do not make nests.

Pet parakeets lay their eggs in a nesting box.

What are mother parakeets called?

This hen parakeet
is inside her nesting box.
She is sitting on her eggs
to keep them warm.

Mother parakeets are called hen parakeets.

Baby parakeets
come from the eggs.
The babies are bare
and have no feathers.
They will grow feathers
when they are bigger.

Why do hen parakeets sit on their eggs?

When the baby parakeets
have their new feathers,
they come out of their box.
Then they try to fly.
Soon they can fly
all around their cage.

Young parakeets
have short tails.

They sit on their eggs to keep them warm.

Tame pet parakeets

Parakeets make good pets.
A parakeet will sit
on your finger
if he likes you.
He will fly around the room
and then come back
to your finger.

Can parakeets fly?

Talking parakeets

If you talk and talk
to a cock parakeet, one day
he may talk back to you.
He has to hear the words
over and over again.
This cock parakeet can say
"Clever Bobby" and
"Good night, Bobby."

Yes. Parakeets can fly.